BLaCK Eyed KidS
Three Months of Hell

By Melissa George
&
Ainsley

Cover Illustration Copyright © 2015 by Melissa George

Cover design Melissa George

Book design and production by Southern Moon Publishing

This is NOT a work of fiction, however the Author has chosen to change names and places in the book to keep the identity of herself and her family private. We respect this right.

ISBN-13:
978-1530906451

ISBN-10:
1530906458

I never believed in anything paranormal. As far as "Unexplained Phenomenon," none of it was real. I had to see it to believe it. Now I don't look at things quiet the same. There are things out there that we don't know about. There are things that are unexplained. And I don't think one should ever need to go looking for these things because they will find you. When the time is right, they are going to find you.

Chapter 1

Let me give you some background before I get started with what happened.

My husband and I purchased a beautiful old farmhouse out in the country. The house was two stories with a big front porch. It was the typical old farmhouse with big rooms and high ceilings. I had always wanted a home like this, and I loved everything about it. My husband Jeff was a real estate agent so when this house came on the market, he immediately took me out to look at it. I fell in love with it before I ever walked inside.

There was a long winding driveway and the house was nestled in the middle of Oak, Pecan, Spruce and Maple trees. The landscape was just breathtaking. There was an old barn out back that would be perfect as a renovated guest house. Just driving up the driveway, I knew I wanted it.

It was early Autumn, so the pecans were just starting to fall. As we walked up to the door, I was thinking of what the house would look like all decorated for the holidays.

The front porch was wrapped with beautiful azaleas and holly bushes. I wanted to put two rocking chairs and a swing on this porch. It would be the perfect place to spend the crisp fall evenings.

The downstairs was spacious and airy. There was a large living room with a fireplace. The living room opened up to a sun room on the back side of the house. This room overlooked the back yard and the woods beyond. I could see a wooden swing from here. It was secured by two large oak trees. I was already anticipating watching the first snowfall from these huge windows.

The dining room was located just off the living room with another fireplace along one wall. This fireplace was a bit smaller with a beautiful hand carved mantle. This would be beautiful for entertaining.

The kitchen was on the back side of the house. It had beautiful large windows over the sink. The cabinets and counter tops looked almost new. It had a center island that would be a perfect place for Jeff and me to have morning coffee. Just off the kitchen was an old fashioned mud room that led into a small porch.

Jeff was laughing about my amazement of the house. He joked about I looked like a country girl in a city mall. I was amazed at everything. He just didn't realize that this house had been my dream since childhood.

It was time to check out the upstairs, and I couldn't wait.

We walked back to the living room to a small hallway. On my right was a full bathroom on my left was a small bedroom and straight ahead was the staircase.

Halfway up, the stairs turned to the right. The landing had a window that overlooked the front porch. I could just picture a small nook underneath this window. I had so many plans for this house and I hadn't even seen all of it! We walked up the rest of the stairs to a hallway with four doors. The upstairs almost ran the length of the house.

The first room to our left was a bedroom with a small closet and two windows. The windows overlooked the front of the house. There was another door by the closet that I could only assume led to a bathroom.

The next room was the master bedroom. It had large windows overlooking the back yard and a small fireplace along one wall. I was thrilled to have a fireplace in our bedroom. How relaxing!

There was a large walk in closet and another door leading to a spacious full bath. This bathroom had been recently renovated. There was a beautiful step-down garden tub that looked big enough for two people. There was also a stand alone shower and a huge vanity.

The next door in the hall was a smaller bathroom. With doors leading to each of the smaller bedrooms.Naturally, I was thinking of fixing these up for the grandkids and using the extra room downstairs as a computer room.

Back out in the hall, Jeff noticed the recessed ladder to the attic. There was no way I was going to explore up there. We would save that for another day. Ever since I was a small child attics had made me nervous. If we bought this house, I would be sure to have Jeff nail it shut.

I knew this house was a bit large for only Jeff and myself. But the grandkids loved to come visit, and I was excited to set the two extra rooms up for them.

Jeff wanted to go look at the yard before it got much later. The sun was setting a bit earlier now than it had the past few months.

We went out through the mudroom into the back yard. The grass had been cut recently and the yard had a cared for look. It made me wonder why someone would give up such a lovely home.

The woods surrounded the back yard. There was a trail that Jeff said led down to the lake. Our property didn't go all the way to the lake. But he said we could use the path if we liked.

Jeff and I purchased our home the following day. And moved in with our two dogs.

Chapter 2

While Jeff was at work I spent my days unpacking and getting the house set up. I had just finished with the kitchen and was about to start on the living room when I saw that our two dogs, Sasha and Samson were pacing from the kitchen to the back door. They were brother and sister, American Pit bull terriers. We kept them in the house most of the time as they were rather large dogs and most people saw them as intimidating. Not to mention that Samson had the problem of wandering off and getting himself into trouble. He would pick up a scent and wander off with his nose to the ground.

I guess it was time to let them out. I had been working for a while without paying attention to the time. I decided to take a break and take them outside. I could sit on the swing and watch them in the back yard.

Jeff had set up two runners for them using the large oak trees. All I had to do was clip their leashes and they would have room to run around but still be confined. Today I would be out with them so they could run free as I supervised.

I opened the back door and both of them ran out into the yard. I was sitting on the swing watching the dogs play when I heard the neighbors kids playing and laughing. The house had to be just across the woods for the voices to sound so clear.

I ran back inside for a minute to grab a glass of tea and my cigarettes. I would take a break while the dogs played for a bit. Heading back out, I opened the back door and Sasha shot in around my legs. This was odd. She wasn't as brave and outgoing as her brother, but she loved being outside. Naturally I went to check on her and she was hiding under the kitchen table. No amount of coaxing would bring her out. Crazy dog. I grabbed my tea and went back out to watch Sampson. When I opened the door, he rushed in almost knocking me down. What in the world was wrong with these dogs?

I left them in the house and went back out by myself. I would have a cigarette and get back to work. As I smoked I would occasionally hear the kids. But the voices were sounding further away now. Maybe the sound was coming from the lake. It was still warm enough in the daytime for a swim.

I went back to unpacking forgetting about the events of the day.

A few days later I took the dogs out and put them on their runners while I arranged the sun room. I had a full view of them and I could work while they enjoyed some outdoor time.

I had been working for a while arranging furniture and assembling a new bookcase. I would look out at the dogs occasionally. They seemed to enjoy being outside. Sasha had laid down under the tree and Samson was busy seeing how far he could reach with the runner. Just as I placed the first books on the shelf, Samson began to bark. It was his warning bark, that you have gotten to close. I looked out to see him digging in with his front legs and pulling on the runner with everything he had. He was focused on the woods to the left of the yard. The direction I had heard the kids. He was determined to get to something. Sasha was jumping and pulling on her lead trying her best to get back to the house.

I dropped the books and rushed through the house. I didn't fear for my dogs at the moment. I had more fear of Sasha hurting herself and Sampson breaking his lead!

I raced out the door and grabbed Samson lead. I had to drag him toward the back door. Each step seemed to be a hundred while he pulled away from me with all strength.

And he is a very muscular dog! I got him into the mudroom and commanded, "Sampson Crate! He went straight into the crate and sat down. I knew he would stay there long enough for me to get Sasha.

Back outside Sasha was still trying to get free to run inside, but now, she was also making small whimpering noises. She practically drug me to the back door and into the house!. I commanded, 'Sasha Crate! She too went right into her crate and sat down, I walked over and latched their crates before I went back outside.

Standing in the back yard now, I couldn't figure out what had upset them so badly. I scanned the tree line all around. I didn't see anything. I stood there straining my ears thinking they could have heard something, but it was deathly quiet. Not even a bird chirped.

All of a sudden, I was overcome with a sense of dread. I felt like something was about to pounce on me. It felt I was being watched by a predator. I was feeling really scared for no reason. I turned and hurried into the house. Once inside I bolted the door and even checked the front to make sure it was locked as well. I knew there was no rational reason for me to feel this way, but I did.

With getting moved in and setting up the house. The episode with the dogs got pushed to the back of my mind.

A few weeks later, I had spent the morning painting upstairs. I had walked the dogs and they were sleeping peacefully in their crates. I thought I would grab a glass of tea and take a break. There was no need for disturbing the dogs, so I went out to the swing to relax by myself.

I was sitting there enjoying the late Autumn sun, and watching the leaves fall. It was so peaceful here. Out of nowhere, I thought that I heard a little girl crying. I stood up and listened to see where the sound was coming from. It was coming from the woods down near the path. I stood there for a minute debating if I should go look or not. The crying sounded so pitiful. Maybe I was mistaken and it was coming from the neighbors. I walked toward the woods in that direction. I could tell now that the sound was coming from the path. I walked down toward the path with the sound growing louder. I had walked about twenty feet down this wooded path when the sound changed from crying to laughter. This sent a wave of pure fear over me! I froze in my tracks. Why would the sound of kids playing have scared me so badly? I wanted to run back toward the house! The laughter sounded as out of place as the crying had. I hurried back to the house not even stopping to grab my tea glass.

Once inside I scolded myself for being so silly. It was just kids playing, nothing more. But I still stayed inside the rest of the day.

That night Jeff and I had gone to bed early. He was tired, but I thought I would read for a little while. I didn't realize it had gotten so late until I heard a knock on the front door.

I looked over at the clock and seen that it was two in the morning! Who in the world would be knocking at this hour?

I climbed out of bed as the knock came again. I started down the steps and stopped at the landing. I didn't see a car in the driveway. But before I could get down the steps whoever was at the door had knocked a third time.

I walked across the living room toward the front door and was consumed with the worst feeling of dread I have ever felt. It was Like I knew there would be a police officer at the door telling me a loved one was dead. I stopped and didn't want to go any further. I waited for the knock to come again, but it didn't. I waited for what seemed like an eternity, but the house was totally silent. I slowly approached the front door and looked out the small sun shaped window.

There was no one there. I unbolted the door and looked out. There was no one out there at all. Feeling confused. I locked the door and went back to bed. I crawled into bed thinking that whoever it was must have thought we weren't home and had walked on over to the neighbor's house. It's funny how our minds will try to rationalize things when there is no obvious answer.

Chapter 3

A couple of weeks had gone by with nothing really happening other than my dogs acting strangely from time to time.

One Saturday Jeff and I were out working in the yards when we heard that pitiful crying again. Samson went nuts and began barking hysterically. While Sasha only whimpered. I had never known them to behave this way because of a child crying. I just kept telling myself that they were in a strange place and just hadn't adjusted yet.

I told Jeff what had happened the last time I heard this cry. So to make me feel better he said we would walk over to the neighbors and introduce ourselves. That way I wouldn't feel so alone here while he was at work. And maybe we could find out where the sound was coming from. I really thought that was a good idea until we approached the woods. I had a sickening feeling of dread wash over me and didn't want to walk through the woods at all. I kept telling myself that Jeff was with me and there was nothing to be afraid of.

It turned out that our neighbors house was much further than we though. I hadn't realized just how much dense wood separated us from their house.

We came out of the woods into their back yard. There was a man out by a barn chopping wood. He looked to be in his early fifties with salt and pepper hair. He wore blue jeans with work boots and a red plaid jacket. The jacket against the background of Autumn trees made him look like something out of a Thomas Kinkade painting. He looked up and saw us, laying down his ax, he threw his hand up. We both waved back as we walked toward him. He approached Jeff, holding his hand out and giving a big welcoming smile.

Mr. Mason, Bob Mason, and Jeff stood there and talked a few minutes while I looked around the yard. It was much like ours, just a bit smaller. As I looked over at the pile of wood he had been working on, I wondered why we hadn't heard him chopping. We should have been able to hear that. Then it occurred to me that there was no way he had kids. Maybe they had been grandkids I quickly scolded myself.

It wasn't long before a short little gray haired woman came to the back door. Bob introduced her as his wife Betty. Betty invited us in for a cup of coffee and a slice of her fresh baked cake.

We chatted with them for a while. Finding out that they had never had children sort of shocked me. I had been positive that all of the children sounds had been coming from here.

Should I ask them if they had heard the sound of children playing? Would my new neighbors think I was crazy? But isn't that why we walked over here, to find out about the kids?

While I was wondering how to go about this, Jeff asked how far the lake was from here. That led to them to discussing how sound travels on the water. Mr. Mason said the trees usually buffered the noises from the lake. That just added to my confusion.

We visited for a bit and headed back home. But not before Betty could wrap us up some cake to take with us.

On the walk back home I had told Jeff that I was certain the kids noises had come from their direction. He reminded me of what Mr. Mason had said. I accepted his explanation, but something just didn't feel right to me.

It was a few days after meeting our neighbors that I decided to walk down to the lake. I crated the dogs instead of taking them with me. Some people found them intimidating, so I thought it would be best to just leave them at home.

It was a beautiful sunny day with a clear blue sky.

The air was a bit cooler today so I was glad I had grabbed a jacket.

I was going across the back yard when I heard the sound of kids playing. I stopped and listened, but I couldn't be sure of where it was coming from. I stood there for a few minutes, but there was just no way of knowing where it was coming from. Maybe If I walked on down to the lake I would be able to figure it out.

The path was very narrow and wound in and around the trees. If two people were walking you would have to walk single file.

I loved the smell of the leaves and the damp earth. I was really enjoying my walk. I rounded a bend in the path and could see the water up ahead between the trees. But what I saw next made me stop in my tracks. There was a little girl standing on the trail facing my direction. Her head was bent down and she had very dark straight hair. Her arms hung down by her sides and the skin of her hands looked ghostly pale. She was wearing, jeans, tennis shoes and a hoodie with the hood pulled up over her head. I was instantly filled with fear. Something about her was off. This didn't feel right at all!

I wanted to turn and run for the safety of my home right then. But I told myself I was being irrational. She was just a child, nothing to fear.

I called out to her and asked if she were OK. She didn't respond and I knew that she had to have heard me. I called out again, and this time, she raised her head to look at me. She raised her head slowly, reminding me of a horror movie.

I was unprepared for what I saw next.
Her face was ashen against the unnaturally black hair. But her eyes, her eyes were coal black. No pupil, no iris, just coal black! Her face was void of any expression. I gasped and stumbled backward as if I had been hit. I have never known such raw terror! My heart was racing and my once strong legs had turned to jello. I turned so quickly I almost fell. I caught my footing and ran! I ran back up the path as fast as I could. With the twists and turns, I am surprised I didn't run headfirst into a tree. Just as I had begun to run. The very moment I turned my back, I could have sworn she said, I'm hungry. Not with any emotion, just those two words. I'm hungry.

I rushed through the back door bolting it behind me. I raced breathlessly into the sun room so I could see if anyone had followed me.

I was looking out the windows at the woods, gasping for breath half doubled over from the pain in my side. What had I just seen? It couldn't have been human! What was that thing?

I stood there scanning the edge of the woods for any glimpse of the child while trying to catch my breath. I wanted to tell Jeff about this when he got home. But I knew I wouldn't. There is just no way he would believe me. This was just too crazy.

I was still pretty shaken up that evening, so when walking the dogs. I went down to the front yard. I still felt uneasy, but it was better than being out back.

That night I awoke to someone pounding on the back door. My first thought was something was wrong with one of the mason's! I jumped up from the bed and flew down the stairs. As I hurried through the kitchen I began to feel that familiar feeling of danger. I stopped and stood there looking at the door. The knock came again, making me jump. My heart was racing and I began to feel nauseous. Suddenly the dogs began to bark and growl from their crates. The sudden noise of it almost caused my legs to buckle. I leaned on the center island to try to calm myself. I was scared to death.

The noise the dogs were making woke Jeff. I didn't know he was up until he spoke. He asked me what was going on. I couldn't control the scream that left my lips!

I spun around to face a startled Jeff. My scream scared him to death. He asked me what in the world was wrong with me as he went to quieten the dogs.

I sat down on the bar stool, to slow my racing heart. My head was beginning to hurt.

Jeff got the dogs settled and came back to the kitchen. He sat down across from me and asked what had happened. I explained to him about the knock on the door waking me up. I told him about the fear that had engulfed me. After explaining everything to him, he got up and opened the door. He walked out onto the porch but there was no one there.

Jeff went back up to bed, but I wanted to sit up for a little longer. My head was really hurting and I wanted to take something for it. There was no way I would ever fall asleep with this headache. I took a couple of aspirin and went out to the sun room. I curled up on the daybed with my book, hoping my headache would subside and the reading would make me sleepy.

As I sat there reading, I saw something out of the corner of my eye. I looked over at the windows and all I could see was my own reflection illuminated by the small table lamp.

I looked back down at my book and it happened again. Something flickered outside, just out of my line of sight. This time, I put the book down and watched.

After a minute or so, I saw it. A small ball of light moving just inside the tree line. I watched it move between the trees. Then it would shoot straight up to the tree tops gliding back down. At times, it would sort of bounce along. It actually looked like this light was playing in the trees.

I turned out the lamp so I could see it better. Then I got up and moved over to the windows. I stood there and watched this strange light for about five minutes. Finally, it moved out of the trees and into the edge of our yard. I could see it better now and it was changing colors. It would sort of evolve from green to sea green to blue. As I watched, it slowly faded and was gone. What in the world had that been? I had never seen anything like it. I had forgotten about my headache as I had watched the light. But all of a sudden it was back worse than ever. I sat back down on the daybed in the dark. I could only sit there until the pain subsided.

Chapter 4

It was a couple of weeks before Christmas now and we had gotten a pretty good snowfall. I was standing in the sun room one afternoon watching the snow coming down when I saw a young boy just inside the tree line. He looked to be about fourteen. As I stood there watching him, I realized that he had been watching me! We didn't have any curtains in the sunroom and it would be easy for anyone to see into the room. It left me feeling really uncomfortable. Why was this young boy just standing there in the snow? And why was he staring at the house? I know teenagers can do some pretty weird things but this was just down right creepy.I thought of calling the police, but I was sure he would be gone by the time they got out here, leaving me looking pretty stupid.

I went out to the kitchen to make myself a cup of coffee. No one could see in there, and it made me feel more secure. As I began to make the coffee I felt another bad headache coming on. I would take something with my coffee and hopefully, feel better soon.

I went out to the sunroom and checked the windows. Just like I thought, the boy was gone. I curled up on the day bed intending to just relax, but I soon fell asleep. Two hours later I woke up feeling much better.

I think Samson knew that I was feeling better too.. He had begun his familiar pacing from the kitchen to the back door. I didn't really want to go out in the cold, but then maybe a short walk would make me feel better. I hadn't taken a walk in the snow yet and I usually looked forward to it. I Grabbed my heavy coat and put Samson's harness on him. I was happy to see that Sasha was still sleeping in her crate. If I did encounter anything Samson would be more protection.

I walked across the snow covered backyard with Samson leading the way. The snow covered landscape was beautiful. I told myself that with the snowfall there was no way anyone would be at the lake. So there was a slim chance of running into that strange kid again.

Samson and I walked the trail weaving in and out of the trees. He was having a wonderful time, stopping every few minutes to mark his territory. He even spooked out a rabbit at one point and I thought we were going on a high speed chase.

As we walked, I noticed my boot had come untied. I stopped to lace it with Samson's lead wrapped around my arm. As I busied myself with my boot, Samson began to let out his low warning growl. Still looking at my boot. My blood ran cold.

Samson was looking down the trail with his hair standing up. I looked to see what he was focused on and there were two kids walking up the trail toward us. They both were wearing Jeans and Hoodies. One looked like the young girl I had seen before. But now there was what appeared to be an older boy with her. They both walked with their heads down. Something in the way they walked just didn't look right.
It seemed as if the atmosphere itself had changed. The woods were no longer peaceful. There was an air of danger now. I quickly started to pull Samson's lead by instinct. Pulling him back toward me. He never lost focus on the kids and he never stopped growling. I knew it would turn into an aggressive bark if the kids kept walking this way.

Did I stand my ground and let them approach, or did I turn and walk away as if I had never seen them? I decided to stand my ground.

My heart was racing and I had begun to sweat. My stomach was tied in knots with fear. As the kids got closer, I called out and ask if everything were OK. I mean, they were kids out in the snow and they were not dressed warmly at all. When I called out, they stopped walking. Almost in unison. The boy raised his head and looked at me. He had the same ashen skin and gaunt face as the girl. His face held no expression. I saw the black eyes about the same time he said, "Let us come home with you." What?! Why would they say this? The young girl was now looking at me too. Their eyes were just solid black orbs. I stumbled backward and tripped on a root. I went down hard! I scrambled to my feet and ran as best I could dragging Samson with me! The fear was overwhelming! All I knew was I had to get away from them as fast as I could. But somewhere, way down deep inside, I thought of bringing them home with me.

As I had once before, I stumbled into the kitchen gasping for breath and terrified! Who were these kids? Were they just playing some kind of sick joke? Were they something Paranormal? I had no clue who or what they were. But I did know that they scared me to death! I stayed inside the rest of the day.

When Jeff got home that evening, I was determined to talk to him. I was going to tell him what had been happening whether he believed me or not. We were sitting in the sunroom watching TV. The fireplace from the living room and the TV in the sunroom were the only light we had. I was wondering how to bring it up when I saw the light out of the corner of my eye. The light was back in the backyard!

I stood up and slowly walked over to the windows. It was there, moving along the tree line again. But this time, there were two!

"Jeff". "Please turn off the TV and come here a minute".

He was as perplexed as I was, watching these balls of light at the far end of our yard. He seemed to be even more shocked when I told him I had watched one of them the other night. I was just about to tell him about the kids. when one of the dogs started making a strange noise. We both went out to the mudroom where the crates were housed. And there was my sweet Sasha, choking! She was frantically pawing at her mouth and clearly in distress!

Jeff raced over to her crate pulling her out onto the floor. She was trying her best to breath, but seemed to be suffocating right in front of our eyes! I was terrified that she would die any second! Tears streamed down my face and my heart was already breaking for the loss of such a sweet, dear friend. He opened her mouth and reach in for the obstruction. But how could she be choking? There was nothing in the dog crates, but their blankets!

I watched as Jeff frantically worked with her! All I could think of was, our baby girl isn't breathing! Then just as fast as It started. She jerked as if she were going into a seizure and gasped, her lungs full of air! She was breathing. I fell on my knees beside Jeff, as Sasha tried to set up. Jeff kept her lying there for a few minutes until he was sure her breathing was OK. I reach out my hand and stroked her face and neck as I spoke softly to her through my tears. Once Jeff was sure she was OK. We took her back into the sunroom with us. After such a scare I think we both just wanted her nearby. By now, the lights were gone. Sasha curled up on the couch beside me as was soon sound asleep.

 I had begun to get another headache. I don't know if it was caused by the stress of the evening. But again, I was taking something before bedtime. This was beginning to seem like a habit.

That night I slept hard from taking medication before bed. I didn't hear the knock on the door.

Chapter 5

I woke up disoriented. The medication still had me groggy.
I lay there in bed wondering what had woken me. The
house was absolutely silent. Then I heard it. Someone
banging on the front door! Bam! Bam! Bam! It vibrated the
whole house! The sudden loud noise caused my adrenalin
to spike. I jumped out of bed and looking over at Jeff. He
was still sound asleep. How in the world did he sleep
through that? Should I wake him? Bam! Bam! Bam! I
hurried to the stairs, wondering what in the world was
going on? Something had to be bad wrong for someone to
be banging on our door in the middle of the night! As I
rushed into the living room, heading for the door. I stopped
abruptly. It all came flooding back. The knocks, that had
happened before with no one being there. The kids in the
woods. The dancing lights. Everything came flooding in all
at once. For the first time I wondered, could all of this be
connected?

Before I could give it any more thought I was hit with a
sickening headache. The pain was unbearable. I stumbled
into the Sun room and lay down on the day bed. At some
point, I had fallen asleep, because that is where I still was
when Jeff came in to kiss me by. I was thankful to be
feeling better now. I guess the extra sleep might have
helped.

I took the dogs out to their runners and made myself some coffee. I thought I would take it easy today and maybe do some reading. I went out to the sunroom and sat down with my coffee.

The dogs were having a blast playing in the snow. They were chasing one another back and forth and kicking up white plumes as they went. I watched them a few minutes before I picked up my book.

I didn't realize I had been lost in my book until Samson's bark brought me back to reality. The clock let me know they had only been out about twenty minutes. But that was plenty long enough with snow on the ground. I put my book down and stood up. That is when I saw the kids. There were three of them now! They were walking away from the yard. What had they been doing? Had they been in my yard? Had they been messing with the dogs? Had they been watching me? I don't know why, but I was sure they had been watching me. I rushed out to get the dogs fearing what might happen to them.

Maybe I just needed to call the police and report these kids. But what could I report? They hadn't actually done anything. I had no proof that they were the ones banging on the door. I had only seen them walking in the woods. They were strange. But so far, not criminals.

None of this made any sense. I wanted to talk to Jeff about everything but I was sure he would think I was Loosing my mind.

I brought the dogs inside and went back to the sun room. Maybe I could find something online that would help me. I didn't have any idea where to even start. I didn't believe in the paranormal, UFO's or anything like that. I always saw that as mistaken identity or people hoaxing for attention. But was this even anything paranormal? I couldn't believe that I was even thinking this way. I sat there staring at the computer screen, not even knowing where to begin looking.

With a sigh, I got up from the computer and went back over to the chair. I sat down and picked up my book. I looked out across the yard, In the split second of my looking up, I thought I saw someone with very ashen skin duck back into the trees!

I made myself a mental note to buy some blinds for these windows. I wasn't liking this open room like I had thought I would.

That evening as Jeff and I sat in the sunroom watching TV, I felt like someone was watching us. I got up and turned off the lamps. But I was still uncomfortable.

I had walked over to the windows a few times and looked out. It didn't occur to me, but Jeff thought I was looking for the dancing lights. He got up and walked over to the window with me. By the time he walked the few steps to where I was, a very low hum had begun. It felt like it came from the atmosphere itself. This sound caused the dogs to go nuts!! They were both barking and growling furiously! Jeff and I exchanged confused looks before rushing to check on the dogs.

Both of the dogs were barking and snarling as if they were ready to attack! They were trying to get out of the crates and had worked themselves into a frenzy. No amount of talking to them was going to calm them down. Jeff opened both crates and released Sasha and Samson. Samson immediately ran to the front door. He threw both feet up on the door as if he wanted to be let out. The barking had not stopped. Sasha headed to the kitchen and backed herself into a corner under the table, shaking and whimpering with her hair standing on end. What had happened to them? I was scared for them as well as myself. What was going on around here?

And still, there was that very low hum. Is this what the dogs were reacting to? Jeff went to the front door and retrieved Samson. This gave me a chance to open the front door and look out.

There was nothing, nor no one out there. I closed the door back and bolted it. Just as I closed the door, the humming stopped.

"What was that"? I asked Jeff.

"It could have been something electrical", he responded. "I'll call an electrician tomorrow."

The dogs stopped as if in unison with the humming. Both of them came back into the sun room with Jeff and me. I walked over to the window and looked out into the darkness. I didn't know how or why, but I was sure the kids had something to do with what was going on in my house. As crazy as that sounded, I was sure of it. More sure now than I had ever been. A part of me never wanted to see them again. But there was a small part of me that wanted to talk to them. I wanted to know why the smallest girl looked so sad. Maybe I would try that the next time I ran into them.

I hadn't noticed it before. But once Jeff, me and the dogs were settled into the sunroom. I felt my headache returning. I felt that this was also tied into it all some how.

Then I saw it, The orange and yellow light bounced across the back yard. As I watched this one move across the yard, two more came out of the woods!

I called Jeff over, and we watched as four lights danced across the lower part of our yard weaving in and out of the trees. I don't know how long we stood and watched them before they faded out. What were they? Jeff thought at first that we were getting some kind of reflection off of the lake. But later he admitted that this was something he just couldn't explain. He was as confused as I was. But they were just beautiful to watch. I like to think of them as fairy lights. But I knew inside, they were somehow a lot more dark and sinister.

I didn't notice until I went to the kitchen to take something for my headache, but the dogs had both gone back to their crates and were sound asleep. This in itself was highly unusual. They would much rather been sleeping on the couches as we watched TV. Jeff latched the crates and we went upstairs to bed.

Chapter 6

Sometime over in the morning, I woke to hear the all too familiar pounding on the front door. I looked over at the clock. It was two thirty in the morning. I knew, there wouldn't be anyone at the door. I had done this too many times before.

Jeff turned on his bedside lamp. "Who in the world could that be"? He asked, getting out of bed.

'There won't be anyone there", I told him.

He looked back at me as if I had lost my mind, as he walked out of the bedroom heading for the stairs. I jumped up and grabbed my robe running to catch up with him. We went down the stairs with me following closely behind. Just as we reach the living room the pounding came again. BAM! BAM! BAM!

Jeff walked over and cut on the porch light. He opened the front door just a few inches, and there stood the three kids! Standing on our porch in the snow with their hoods pulled down low over their heads. All three of them were looking down.

'We're cold", said the older one.
"May we come in"? Asked the middle of the three.
"Daddy will be here soon", said the little girl.

Jeff opened the door wider for them to come in.
"Jeff don't!", I screamed.

"They're just kids Ainsley", He responded.

My head began to pound as the three kids walked into my living room. Jeff closed the door and turned to look at me. His nose had begun to bleed! I ran out to the kitchen to grab a cold cloth, and that's when I noticed that the dogs had not barked at all. I wet the cloth and took it back to Jeff, who was now sitting on the couch. The three kids were still standing in the same spot just inside the door.

I stepped around them to get to Jeff, diverting my eyes. I didn't want to look at their dead ashen skin. I thought I might scream if I saw those black soul less eyes. The quiet hum had started again.

I handed Jeff the wet cloth and went back out to check on the dogs. I turned the light on in the mud room, and to my horror, the crates were empty! The doors were still closed, but they were empty.

I knew that was the last thing Jeff had done before going to bed. Where we the dogs? My heart was racing and I was terrified! I raced to the door and flung it open calling their names. It had begun to snow again and there wasn't even a footstep showing on the porch. I knew this too was tied in with those kids.

I went back out into the living room to find Jeff sitting there with his head in his hands. As if he had a horrible headache. The kids still stood near the door. I cannot explain the fear I felt just seeing these three things standing in my house. I knew now what they wanted. They wanted us dead. That is the bottom line. What other reason could they be here?

I asked Jeff to please come with me. I wanted him to go help me find the dogs and we would leave. I would leave them standing there in my house as long as me and Jeff got out with our dogs. Just then the older one turned and leered at me as if he had read my mind!! I screamed for Jeff to come on, as he slowly slumped over on the couch. Oh dear God! He needed help!

I turned and ran for the sunroom! I had to call 911. But what would I say? What would I tell them?

The dispatcher answered the phone and I screamed out," It's my husband! Please help him"!

She was asking more questions as I threw the phone on the day bed and ran back to Jeff. My front door was standing wide open with the snow blowing in. The kids were gone. The hum had stopped and the kids were gone.

I tried my best to wake Jeff, but I couldn't! Dear God, please let him wake up! Please God! I prayed feverishly for God to spare my husband, my best friend. To just make things normal again.

As the hot tears streamed down my face, I caught a glimpse of something moving. Sasha was doing a belly crawl into the front door as if she were scared to death. I jumped up and ran to her. She was alive! My baby girl was alive. But I couldn't be happy just yet. Samson and Jeff still weren't OK. I couldn't be happy until I had my family again. Dear God please make this all OK.

Sasha slowly stood up at the sound of my voice, but still she shied away. I moved closer to her and then I saw Samson! It was a fluttering moment of sweet relief. But it left as fast as it came. Samson stood on the porch as if afraid to come in. I knelt down and coaxed him to me.

Just as I got Samson in the door safely, I stood up to close it, I didn't get it closed before I saw a tall man dressed in all black, with the same ashen skin. He was standing in my front yard. The porch light illuminated him. He was looking at me with those cold black eyes. In a split second those eyes turned a fiery red as if a fire burned in his very soul. Then, like the dancing lights, he just vanished!

I heard the sirens in the distance, I knew they were coming for Jeff. I slowly closed the door and stood there to wait. I knew there were no need for them to hurry.

Chapter 7

It was a beautiful sunny day. I actually needed to wear dark sunglasses against the glare of the snow. Jeff would Love it. He would have wanted to take the dogs for a walk. I thought this as I lay three red roses on top of his casket. One from me, one from Samson and one from Sasha. Samson and Sasha sat by my chair with their heads lowered as if they too grieved for Jeff.

Jeff died of an aneurysm on his brain. It ruptured that night, killing him instantly. They promised me that he didn't suffer. At this point, that is all I could ask.

Me and my dogs are staying with our daughter now. I will live with her until I think I can do it on my own. I wont go back to that house. Our kids boxed everything up and put the house up for sale. It had been my dream, as well as my nightmare.

I still feel them watching me. I know they are close by. They are just waiting for the right time. There is nothing I can do but wait.

I know now, what we encountered. I know what killed Jeff. Some people call them "the black eyed kids." Please believe me, they are NOT kids. They are evil, pure, raw evil. And they want your very soul. Your death, is what they come for.

I don't know why things turned out the way they did. I still have more questions than answers. One day, I would like to find the previous owners of that property. I feel like they may know something. I think they too had an experience. One day, when the time is right, I want to look for the answeres to my questions. I want to know how and why this happened to us, and just maybe, with that knowledge, I can help someone else.

Thank you for reading.

May God Bless You.

40390717R00027

Made in the USA
San Bernardino, CA
19 October 2016